Table of Contents

Preface 9
Twining 13
Little Girl Dreaming 15
They Already Know 17
Equivocation 19
Early Admissions 21
Saudade 23
Pink Coded Girl 25
Court Side 27
One Size Fits All 29
Girl's Girl 31
Kismet 33
C.N.S 35
Tryhard 37
Sunday Services 39
Privacy Policy 41
Southern Hospitality 43
Bookwyrm 45
American Girl Dolls 47
Holier Than Thou 49
The Summer I Got Sick 51
Language Learning Models 53
Vertigo 55
I Am Not Trying To Change You 57
Sorry for accidentally ripping your maps 59
"Peacekeeper" 61
Little Girls Who Don't Know How to Communicate 63

I Bite 65
Depersonalization 67
I AM SOBER 69
Wanderlust 71
The Girl From Nowhere 73
Secondhand Platonic Love 75
Irish Goodbye 77
I Can't Be Friends With Boys Anymore 79
People Pleaser 81
Tell-All 83
Narcissus 85
I'll Wake Up At Six A.M. and Wonder Where You Are 87
Galentines 89
Solitary Confinement 91
Cheyenne 93
Acknowledgements 95

Praise for To All The Girls I've Loved Before

Poetry often addresses romantic heartbreak, but rarely does it touch on the heartbreak of losing platonic friends—these poems fill that gap in a beautiful, poignant way. Anger, grief, and soul-wrenching questions drip from the pages of this deeply personal collection. Get some highlighters and tissues ready for this one, folks—you're going to need them.

—Amelia E. Clawford, author of
All There Is To Know About Frogs

In her debut poetry collection, Sera Amoroso walks us through self-discovery paired with the losses and gains of growing up. It's as heartwarming as it is heart-wrenching.

—Nathaniel Luscombe, author of
My Roots Can't Leave the Ground

To All The Girls I've Loved Before is a razor-sharp examination of lost friendships, complex family dynamics, and chronic illness from the perspective of an autistic, adopted military kid. Amoroso weaves subtle humor with devastating insight that will resonate with anyone who's been told they're "too much." This is a fantastic debut poetry collection!

—Ellie Ember, author of *Paper Castles*

In To All the Girls I've Loved Before, Sera Amoroso delivers a scathing denouncement of neurotypical society and how often it fails its most vulnerable members. Amoroso mourns the isolating experience of growing up autistic with visceral vulnerability, while maintaining a defiant spark and dedication to self-love. These poems are firecrackers, lighting up the pages in a tragic, resilient, furious ode to anyone who has ever dared to believe in the promises they were given.

—MJ Anthony, author of *Tending Clay; Unearthing Stars*

Like a good meal, To All The Girls I've Loved Before is easy and pleasurable to consume, but sticks to your ribs for awhile. Amoroso masterfully honors the ghost of one's past that aren't easy to shake, while simultaneously letting us know everything will be alright.

—K. Rose, *Advanced Reader*

Sera Amoroso

To All The Girls I've Loved Before

Copyright © 2025 by Sera Amoroso (Beyond the Stars Press)
Originally Published 2025 in Tampa, Florida USA by Beyond the Stars Press

All rights reserved. No part of this book may be reproduced, stored in a retrieval system, or transmitted in any form or by any means—electronic, mechanical, photocopy, recording, scanning, or other—except for the use of brief quotations in critical reviews or articles without prior written permission of the publisher. This book and its cover may not be licensed to train AI, or used by AI in any manner.

This is a work of fiction. Names, characters, places, and incidents either are the product of the author's imagination or are used fictitiously. Any resemblance to actual persons, living or dead, events, or locales is entirely coincidental.

ISBN: 978-1-7372310-5-9

First Edition—September 2025

Scripture quotations taken from The Holy Bible, New International Version®, NIV®. Copyright © 1973, 1978, 1984, 2011 by Biblica, Inc. Used with permission of Zondervan. All rights reserved worldwide.

Cover art by Erelah Emerson
Interior formatting by Riley Perrie

To all the friends I've loved and lost, the ones who've stayed, and the ones I've yet to meet.

Preface

I want to say that this book is not just poetry or free verse prose, it's memories. I started writing novels at fourteen years old, and when I was ready to publish at sixteen, I chose a pen name. Not only did it grant me online safety, but also privacy. Emotionally speaking, this anthology is an expression of the grief and pain associated with my childhood. Some of the titles even reference disorders I was actually diagnosed with.

I grew up in a dysfunctional and sometimes abusive environment and struggled with depression and anxiety from a very young age. I was adopted when I was four years old. My parents never hid that fact from me, or that my twin brother and I were put into the foster care system as soon as we were born. This, along with my parents' divorce, made me develop an attachment disorder when I was twelve. I often struggled with my own identity; I had trouble making friends due to undiagnosed autism (which I wouldn't be diagnosed with until I was 15) and being a military kid. My parents also put no effort into educating me about the culture I came from.

I would describe my situation as being in a loving but toxic family. While I was cared for and had an objectively good life, my emotional and health needs were not being met. Due to being late diagnosed, I developed fibromyalgia and later chronic fatigue syndrome because of constant masking. I also learned that I had alexithymia, a neuropsychological phenomenon that caused me to have difficulty recognizing, describing, and reacting to my own emotions, as well as those of the people around me.

The reason I'm prefacing this book with this story is not because I hate myself, my life, or my parents. While I was low contact with my family while writing this collection, I know that their faults do not reflect on me, and I've slowly started re-establishing a relationship with them.

I've written this, not because I'm still angry, but because I'm not anymore. This book is a symbol of my healing. My words may seem childish, or sad, and that's because they are, because I was childish and sad. Just because I've healed, doesn't mean I'm never sad, and I often mourn the person I never got to be.

So, to all of you, this is for your inner child. For everyone who could never express themselves in a coherent manner, to all your midnight scribbles, and scrambled thoughts. To all the people who made me who I am (good or bad), I love you.

One who has unreliable friends soon comes to ruin, but there is a friend who sticks closer than a brother.
—Proverbs 18:24 NIV

Twining

Maybe in ten years I will look back on this
And say "that made sense"
But how strange it is to see you grow up without me
To watch your life in pictures
And unread texts

Little Girl Dreaming

And I will kill her off
Zealous for a break
Altar kneeling for a moment
Lying in a cage
I will cut the rope
Everlasting, still the waves

Cliffside shooting stars
Hell is on the way
Every shattered glass
Yelling at the stage
Ending on a high note
Never understand
Nighttime restoration
Evergreens buried under sand

Several people waiting
Eyeing distant storms
Racing to the summit
Angry evermore

Merriment in danger
Evening tea time on the porch
Running past the corn fields
On the way to scorn
Nickles traded in
Endless til the morn'

They Already Know

It's much ado about nothing
Crying over nothing
Skin as paper thin as I can manage
Without ripping, without tearing out my hair
Over people, over places, I wish I didn't care
I can feel it in my chest, like I ripped my own heart out
The air of indifference, of being too different
Without a word coming out of my mouth

Equivocation

Words on words on words, written red on the windowpanes. Each and every letter carved in wood, paid in pain. It's always over before it even began, words forever misconstrued. Too much, too little, never just right, only halfway, and slightly too rude.

Early Admissions

I am tired of knowledge,
Of knowing, of just getting by
My therapist thinks it's okay to see me twice
A month, says I'm so self aware
I already know that, and I know it's unfair

Saudade

There is a dreadful aching in my bones
Perhaps I have wanted too much
I am okay with split ends and spilled ink
With skinned knees and torn blankets

But, I think I might be sick
of all my blue ribbons and framed papers
Scrawled-in-margins letters to myself
Future people have passed me by on the stairs

And maybe when I am half-way healed,
Or almost full, then I will just be
Not clawing to achieve, just so I can say
I've done it

Pink Coded Girl

How many times did I lay on the pool deck
talking to you?
How many times did you stay over, hushed
voices under the moon?
How many times did I walk in your house,
bake cakes, help you clean your room?

How many times have you texted me
these past few months?
How many times have you ran?
I know you're finding yourself,
but, come on, man.

Manic pixie dream girl
I like to call it "halfway friends"
Road trips and heartaches
Watching movies at 1 am
Never truly seeing each other

And maybe one day you'll be famous
Maybe it'll be me
Maybe I'll meet you at some flashy event
And we can finally talk about everything

Though I know you'll never see this
Let's be real, you don't read
I like to think you're doing well
You always did, eventually

Court Side

I would say I was privileged in some ways. I got to travel, got to learn, got to write. I would say I suffered in other ways. Call's coming from inside the house, guys. I'm not aware of my body without the pain. I am aware of the faces you make when you think I'm not looking. I've been told I'm off-putting, I know. Uncanny valley kind of know it all, like it's okay to treat me as less than. Suffocating when you don't pick up my calls. Maybe it's middle child syndrome or maybe you're just self-centered. I wrote twelve letters to you and burned them in the very same yard you used to run around with me in. I'm used to being the one who moved away, but I'm glad you did. I'm glad I deleted your number. I'm glad your sister apologized for you. I don't like your family, I've never liked your mother, and I'm not sure why I latched onto you. But I owe you one thing, and that is the spite I threw out. I pushed myself forward so you wouldn't leave me behind. You still did, but now I'm ahead.

One Size Fits All

I forgot the way the story goes, but from what I can remember
I had handed you my heart and you gave me a letter
Said, it's patience, it's the waiting, it's investing in my time
Now it's tanking, it's all wasting, washing away with the tide
I like to think we're friends and you like to think I'm easy
I'm still working on myself but I can't get past the critiquing
How can you, no, how dare you benefit from my bleeding

Girl's Girl

Performative activism in pastel colors and beat up sneakers
Someone funny, kind, a fake, a safe space
It's not a boundary, the way you always offer help but never follow through
Protecting your peace
There for the good times and gone for convenience
Overcompensating anxiety with people pleasing
Neither good nor bad and always troubling
Talking behind my back and hers

Kismet

I am going places
Maybe the hospital,
but hey, that is a place

Maybe I'll find myself in
a school or a church
Or I'll find my way back
home

Is it that I cried for help
too many times; you just
thought I was crying wolf

You don't owe me anything,
but didn't you sign the contract?
You paying in cold, hard cash or
empathy?

C.N.S

I want to say that it is okay to outgrow people, because there is a you-shaped hole in my heart, half overgrown with new tendons. I want to say that I do not mind being low maintenance, never talked to, never put first, there to lend a shoulder or an ear. There are exceptions, I know. I want to say that I'm fine with glass shards in my throat, glass hearts in my hands. I want to allow myself to be halfway empty and content with those I've left behind; I am never satisfied, and I am thinking way too much. It's not a matter of character, or that I'm not liked. It's not a reflection on myself, or on you. It's not that I don't see the good in people all the time or that I'm too close-minded. It's not the mismatched ratio of empathy to lack thereof. It's simply that we're not meant to be.

Tryhard

This everflowing kindness is tiring
My lungs are filled with sand and yet
I breathe; I wonder; I scream
Is this ignorance? Or am I truly just
as selfish as you think?

Can you meet me in the middle?
Can you try to cross the line?
Can you hold out your hand first?
Must the job always be mine?

Can I not be angry? Can I not be sad?
Can I not outsource my peace from He
who understands? If this is how the world
shall work, then I don't want to be an ant
whose purpose is to always be following.

Sunday Services

Give unto Caesar what is Caesar's
and give unto God what is God's.
It is always obey your parents,
never do not provoke your children.
The ringing in my ears combines
your yelling and the slightly too loud
sound of the guitar.

And maybe if I wasn't wearing earplugs
or rocking in my seat. Maybe if you didn't
push for me to stand up there and sing.
Maybe if I was healthy, or you didn't
see yourself in me.
Maybe if I was younger and I wasn't forced
to scream.
Maybe I could just sit there, and just be.

Privacy Policy

No amount of apologies
will cover what you said to me.
Spilling all my secrets.
Gossiping about my struggling.

Twisting all my choices based
on perceived disobedience.
"It's just to keep you safe."
While you tell all of your friends
that I'm not strong in my faith.

I want to say that I outgrew
the anger, but I didn't.
Forced myself to face the fact
that I might not be forgiven.

Southern Hospitality

Sweet tea in the fields behind the parking lot
Some girls only pick up the phone when there's panicking
It's too much work, too inconvenient
Pet projects you blame for catastrophes
Still, I'm watching you lie through pictures
Deleting old photos and poems I wrote
Shredding handwritten thank you notes

Bookwyrm

Is this pure escapism?
Back pressed to the door
Drowning out the screaming
With a dragon and a sword

I crawled under my bed
Into another life
Envisioning myself as a songbird
With black feathers and a knife

American Girl Dolls

I want to feel vindicated instead of victimized,
but I just feel sad. I know you did your best,
making do with what you had. I'm sorry, for all
the times we fought. Still, gifts don't make up
for all the pain you wrought. You let me get
shut up in a box. A doll that you could shape.
Maybe if you'd listened to me then, it wouldn't
be too late.

Holier Than Thou

I have strived to say that I am holy
but the emptiness consumes.
Still, my ears echo with dove calls
as I sit motionless next to you in the pews.
Is this a tomb? Am I still dead in my ways?
Is the cross I wear around my neck
a symbol of decay?
I'm not holy. Not without bloody hands
and feet. I don't want to claim to be.
Stained glass windows swim in circles; I
will die on my knees.

The Summer I Got Sick

Heavy bones, lifted hearts.
Chalk art on the sidewalk.
I can count the times I got
the blisters, but for bruises;
I don't know where to start.

Half-full glass of grapefruit
juice spilled on the tablecloth.
I can't remember when they
started; only that I'm lost in
shaky hands and headaches,

that never fully go away.

Language Learning Models

I am trying so hard
And it feels like you hate me
Every word out of my mouth
Sets up a catastrophe
I don't want to be pushy
Or selfish or mean
Adapting the way you speak
Like a machine

Vertigo

It's been 2 hours
Sometimes 20
Sometimes none
Skip out on my bed so I can
Learn to balance
Being perfect
Always landing on my feet

Doing just to say I've done it
Doing for relief
I try to swear off coffee
and spill it on my Bible study notes
Nearly break down in the classroom
Bite my tongue and choke

I Am Not Trying To Change You

I am trying to be kind.
Keep in mind:
It's your first time living,
and I'm allowed to cry

Placing emphasis on tone
across a hundred miles.
You don't really feel that way;
I'm just projecting.

I fear that I'm not valued here.
Can't feel my hands; scream in
my ears. Community dues are
paid for in the burden you
place on others. It's meant to
be shared.

Sorry for accidentally ripping your maps.

I wondered then if you only stayed
because there was nowhere else
to go. If picture frames on mantles
reflected from yours into my home.
It's funny, now, finding out, your mother
lectured mine. Sitting in abandoned
parks just to pass the time. We are ever
changing, still yet to know. Daily
meetings turn to monthly, but there's
always space to grow.

"Peacekeeper"

I'm seeing you now as who you are:
Someone who never cared. Who centers
people she falls in love with over those
who were always there. And sure, have
your person, have your cake and eat it
too. But you're the reason we keep leaving,
why you're calling it just a joke. Yeah, I left
the same way your old friends did because
you won't put out the fires while complaining
about the smoke.

Little Girls Who Don't Know How to Communicate

I think I was twelve, or fourteen, or
seventeen, or twenty.
I think I was six or four or two or
zero.

I think I know this isn't normal, but
my heart is sealed with glue.
I think it's called kintsugi, but I think
I did it wrong.

I know the callouses didn't appear
overnight, but they're not from cello strings.
I know I don't hate myself, but I think you
might hate me.

I think I'm kind and sweet and caring and
you think I'm brash and rude and angry.
I know there's a mistranslation somewhere;
But I think it's crushed up on the driveway.

I Bite

I am so full of hate
I want to rip off my skin
I am so full of anger
I want to tear out my eyes
Don't patronize me
I understand it perfectly
You are making fun of me
Just to laugh when I lash out

Depersonalization

I never wanted to be pretty.
Changing things to be as
more than just a body. More
than whispered words to other people

Maybe it's self sabotage:
the way I shaped myself.
But would it be so terrible
to expire on the shelf?

Laughter makes my ears bleed;
from clothes to shoes to makeup.
Constantly commenting
on every part of my make up.

To be loved is to be seen but
it's dark inside of the screen.
I never wanted to be pretty;
I never wanted to be mean.

I AM SOBER

It will be 2 or 5 or maybe 12 years until you learn that the same people who listen to you with carefully worded speeches about how they love you, will be the same people who leave you stranded.

It will be 3 or 6 or 10 months until you finally get clean and throw out all your kitchen scissors and lock the knives away; no one ever noticed and you had to make the decision to stay.

It will be 1 or 4 or 11 days that you have to take a break. Life will not pause for you, so you must sit up and smile and listen and lend a hand to people who you know will not be there tomorrow.

It will be a lifetime. But it will be okay.

Wanderlust

I told you once that I wanted you to be my maid of honor. Now someone else will take your place. That is, if I have a wedding.

I told you that you'd always have a shoulder to cry on. Thanks, by the way, for making me a liar.

I switched all our plans around. I have new people to travel with. I'll share a cake in Italy with someone else on my 25th.

As I outgrow the people I swore to protect, I wonder if the boots I wore until they fell apart reflect my inability to change.

If never fully getting unpacked, keeping a book in my backpack, learning pieces of new languages will be my undoing.

I don't know if I ever grew up.

The Girl From Nowhere

I do not know if it's the not knowing
The storm, the bitten nails, the name
Or the aching inside

I don't know her or who she might've been
I scrape at my throat and my eyes
I do not know if it's the not knowing

There's an odd shaped hole in my journal
In pictures, the head torn off. Is it the desperation?
Or the aching inside

I have torn the connection out with my own teeth
Not my choice first, but now mine
I do not know if it's the not knowing

My place is among spilled tea stains on old books I used to love
As much as it is in rice I did not wash. Is that my lungs
Or the aching inside

I've given up on learning, on growing, on feeding
I do not know if it's the not knowing
Or the aching inside

Secondhand Platonic Love

And we will never be 17,
sitting in the back of a
truck at 9 p.m. ever again.
We will never be eating
sandwiches, laughing
about game night and
talking about where we
want to go to college.
We will never be that
full of laughter, sparkling
eyes under twinkling stars,
gossiping about coworkers.
I will give you away, and it
will be bittersweet, and I
don't think I will ever love
another person the way that
I loved you.

Irish Goodbye

I saw you at my best friend's graduation
Why'd you look so different?
Cut your hair and changed your clothes
If you were happy, then I'd get it
But you seemed tired
Lost all your color
I've been there, I understand
I wish I made a scene, wish I screamed
at you for never giving a reason
Just one day leaving
Washed away with the sand

I Can't Be Friends With Boys Anymore

Glass tongue, black eyes,
smoking on the roof.
I hear you say you
stay friends with friends
of friends just because
they didn't hurt you. Huh?

You try to cross my
boundaries: make me
stay and make me
drink. I throw the gifts
away, and throw up in
the sink. Still hate it.

It's okay to not support,
it's really not a race. But,
man, I know you hate on
me because I don't act
my age. You don't either.

You laugh about the fact
that I am years ahead, while
painting 3D models and trying
to make sense. I don't think
you even know what you're learning.

Why's it fair that I have to
be mature? I'm praying for
you, really, but I can't stand
this anymore. Some of you
need to learn to clean up
after yourselves.

I stay up late and try to join
in on your games. I still don't
get it, and your explanations
are in vain. It's not funny that
you keep killing me.

Sure, there are exceptions to
every rule. But maybe it is true.
Maybe guys can't be friends with
girls. Or maybe you're just cruel.
Please delete my number.

People Pleaser

I can write a novel but I can't read a room
I tried to speak your language but I
couldn't interpret you
It's sick to know that I'd still show up when
you didn't
Penciled in my exit on the calendar in your
kitchen
Sure, I'm not a perfect woman, but you're
no real prize either
Paid your way in fool's gold, different values
over ways of validating tickets

Tell-All

I will remember everything; dumping gallons of blood just to hold a grudge.
Passively ripping out pages, expressionless stabbing of pillows.
I want to call you out by name, but

I.

Know.

Better.

Be the bigger person, Sera, it's fine.
Take up space while they still let you, give them grace, they don't understand you, shutting off your mic, you're too loud. You talk too much.

I.

Know.

Better.

Burying secrets in the margins of the "poetry" I wrote. Hid your name on the page so I can laugh and gloat. I wish I was angrier. I wish I tore into everybody. You deserve it, yet

I.

Know.

Better.

That's too many battles; put some back. I need to rest. Non-stop, the amount of work I do, just to prove myself. I'm smart enough. But I could always get higher, go further, run faster, I am running out of time.

I.

Know.

Better.

I'm going to cut off my tongue. I'm going to disappear into the forest. I built that community center with my own bare hands, I'm allowed to tear it down. It was for a reason, and

I.

KNOW.

BETTER.

Narcissus

There will be no village unless you make one. Let it all get burned down. The foundation is all that matters, let it all be ruins for now. It is okay to struggle: take some time to self-reflect. If you fall in love with your own image, you'll have to tear your face off to rebuild what was left.

I'll Wake Up At Six A.M. and Wonder Where You Are

I keep scrolling through our texts
and selecting all the patterns;
Realizing I always reach out first.

Will this be forever? I don't know.
You send me videos but we won't make
new plans. I'm more excited to take
pictures, to show you I'm doing well.

I keep planning like you'll stick around.
I know you will, I know you do—why'd
the effort disappear?

I make decisions based on myself,
not if you'll be at my events. You
say you're cheering from the sidelines,
but I don't even get a text.

We both have new people,
but I'll still make the time.
Traditions fade into bimonthly letters as we
try to make the drive.

Galentines

Revelations scrawled in notebook margins
I've forgotten how to breathe
All of my successes claimed alone
Hidden in the weeds

It's not like you don't celebrate
I'll mention it in passing
Spend more time in the comfort
Buried resentment under laughing

Reconciled my abandonment
You don't have to always be there
Holidays turn to date nights
I wish I was unaware

Solitary Confinement

I'm worried that my questioning is heresy
I wonder if I'll ever truly know
I'm sure that I really am the poison
Acidic, burning holes in my own throat
I've given up on finding home in others
I'm terrified that I'll always be alone
I took a knife to my old friendship bracelets
Following the emptiest of roads

Cheyenne

I grieve her. She will never
exist again. Sandwiched
between names that
will always be preferred.
I will never fully unpack the box
that she sits in; the reasons
I get ready to run every
two to three years.

I grieve her. And it's bitter irony
that the one place I remember
with semi-sweet memories
killed me inside a little bit.
I will never like hospitals, or
courtrooms, or bicycles, or
cities, no matter how long
I exist inside of them.

I grieve her. She didn't
get to know her language,
or her country, or her last name.
Sacrificed for better opportunities;
but I look at pearl rosaries on
the internet and wonder if
I'd be the same if she was
still alive.

I grieve her. Not in the sense of
I wish she was still here,
but rather that I wish I never knew
about her dirty blonde hair,
her entitled attitude with tying shoes,
her happiness in stacking blocks
against the wall.

I grieve her. I worry about her
misspoken words and bubbly
laughter. I reminisce on
losing her. I do not want to
see her in photo albums. I
do not hate her. Still, part
of me wants her to know that
she is safe. Cradled in between
whispers and signatures on
wrinkled paper.

I grieve her. I grieve for her
and the sisters she never
met and never will.

I grieve her.

Acknowledgements

When I was writing this collection, I worried a lot of what my parents would think of it. In fact, I put off publishing it, solely because I was scared of how they'd react to it. Despite years of therapy, I don't think I ever truly stopped thinking about what they'd say about my writing. It was only in discussing this collection with two of my close childhood friends that I learned about how they saw my life from the outside.

In fact, one of the funniest memories I have from going home during college is sitting in the car with them and hearing about how they both reacted to the way I was treated by both my mother, and my church community, and the way they talked about it with their mothers. Though, this is not to hate on my mother as I have reconciled with her; her life was difficult, and being a single mother is something that I never want to be. She did the best that she could with what she was given, and I am so grateful for that, despite everything.

So, I want to thank Ellie for putting up with all the poems I sent her at random times during the day. I want to thank my best friend for all the stories and outside perspectives, and especially for helping me have the courage to talk about everything. I want to thank my community for being such incredible supporters and friends. I want to thank God, for being the reason I was able to pull myself out of the situation I was in and giving me the strength to forgive the people who inspired this collection. And, of course, I want to thank my family. I love you.

About the Author

Sera Amoroso is the self-published author of The Makria Cycle. She's a freelance editor, cosplayer, linguist, tea enthusiast, and avid reader. She spends most of her time at home with her dog, Minnie.

She has been writing stories since she was ten years old. Ever since she got her hands on books such as The Lord of the Rings, and Ender's Game, she wanted to publish one of her own.

Torsion, her debut novel, kicks off The Makria Cycle trilogy. She's also been featured in the anthology Aphotic Love, and the 2024 edition of The Dragon Bone Journal. When she's not writing, she can be found reading, creating languages, and playing games with friends.

Visit Sera at seraamoroso.com or
@seraamoroso on Instagram

www.ingramcontent.com/pod-product-compliance
Lightning Source LLC
Chambersburg PA
CBHW060406080526
44583CB00012B/488